EMMANUEL JOSEPH

Style with Soul, How Fashion Can Honor the Earth and Uphold Ethics

Copyright © 2025 by Emmanuel Joseph

All rights reserved. No part of this publication may be reproduced, stored or transmitted in any form or by any means, electronic, mechanical, photocopying, recording, scanning, or otherwise without written permission from the publisher. It is illegal to copy this book, post it to a website, or distribute it by any other means without permission.

First edition

This book was professionally typeset on Reedsy. Find out more at reedsy.com

Contents

1	Chapter 1: The Intersection of Fashion and Ethics	1
2	Chapter 2: The Environmental Impact of Fast Fashion	3
3	Chapter 3: Sustainable Materials and Their Benefits	5
4	Chapter 4: The Power of Ethical Brands	7
5	Chapter 5: Embracing a Minimalist Wardrobe	9
6	Chapter 6: The Role of Fashion Activism	11
7	Chapter 7: Circular Fashion: Closing the Loop	13
8	Chapter 8: The Rise of Slow Fashion	15
9	Chapter 9: Ethical Fashion and Cultural Heritage	17
10	Chapter 10: The Role of Technology in Ethical Fashion	19
11	Chapter 11: The Importance of Consumer Awareness	21
12	Chapter 12: The Economics of Ethical Fashion	23
13	Chapter 13: Building an Ethical Fashion Brand	25
14	Chapter 14: The Future of Ethical Fashion	27
15	Chapter 15: Ethical Fashion for All	29
16	Chapter 16: Ethical Fashion and Personal Style	30
17	Chapter 17: Conclusion: Style with Soul	32

1

Chapter 1: The Intersection of Fashion and Ethics

Fashion is not just about looking good; it's about doing good as well. The industry has the power to shape societal norms, influence behaviors, and create trends that resonate with the values we hold dear. Ethical fashion is about making choices that honor the earth, respect human rights, and promote sustainability. This chapter explores the intersection of fashion and ethics, highlighting the importance of aligning our style with our values.

The journey towards ethical fashion begins with awareness. Consumers are becoming more conscious of the impact their choices have on the environment and on the lives of those who produce their clothes. Understanding the supply chain, from raw materials to finished products, is crucial in making informed decisions. Ethical fashion brands prioritize transparency, ensuring that every step of the process is accounted for and meets high standards of sustainability and fairness.

Sustainability is at the heart of ethical fashion. The industry is notorious for its environmental footprint, with fast fashion contributing to pollution, waste, and resource depletion. Ethical fashion seeks to minimize this impact by using eco-friendly materials, reducing waste, and promoting practices that conserve resources. This chapter delves into the various sustainable practices that are transforming the fashion industry, from organic cotton to recycled fabrics.

Another key aspect of ethical fashion is social responsibility. The people who make our clothes often work in poor conditions, with low wages and little protection. Ethical fashion brands are committed to ensuring fair labor practices, providing safe working conditions, and supporting the communities involved in production. This chapter examines the human side of fashion, emphasizing the need for brands to uphold the rights and dignity of their workers.

2

Chapter 2: The Environmental Impact of Fast Fashion

Fast fashion is characterized by rapid production and consumption, leading to a cycle of constant turnover in stores and closets. While this model has made fashion more accessible, it comes at a significant environmental cost. This chapter explores the environmental impact of fast fashion, shedding light on the hidden consequences of our shopping habits.

One of the most pressing issues is the sheer volume of waste generated by fast fashion. Clothes are often designed to be worn a few times before being discarded, leading to mountains of textile waste in landfills. Synthetic fibers, which are prevalent in fast fashion, take hundreds of years to decompose, releasing harmful chemicals into the environment in the process. This chapter highlights the importance of reducing waste and promoting a culture of reuse and recycling in fashion.

Water consumption is another major concern. The fashion industry is one of the largest consumers of water, with processes like dyeing and finishing requiring vast amounts of this precious resource. The chapter discusses the impact of water-intensive practices and the need for more sustainable alternatives. Innovations such as waterless dyeing and closed-loop systems are paving the way for a more water-conscious fashion industry.

Chemical pollution is a byproduct of many fashion production processes.

The use of dyes, finishes, and other chemicals can result in the release of toxic substances into waterways, affecting both ecosystems and human health. This chapter examines the efforts being made to reduce chemical usage and promote safer alternatives. Eco-friendly dyes, organic fabrics, and natural finishes are gaining traction as brands seek to minimize their chemical footprint.

Finally, the chapter addresses the carbon footprint of the fashion industry. From transportation to production, fashion contributes to greenhouse gas emissions, exacerbating climate change. Ethical fashion aims to reduce this impact through practices such as local production, carbon offsetting, and the use of renewable energy. This chapter outlines the steps that can be taken to create a more climate-friendly fashion industry.

3

Chapter 3: Sustainable Materials and Their Benefits

Choosing the right materials is a cornerstone of ethical fashion. Sustainable materials not only reduce environmental impact but also offer unique benefits in terms of quality, comfort, and durability. This chapter explores the world of sustainable fabrics, highlighting their advantages and the innovations driving their adoption.

Organic cotton is a popular choice for ethical fashion brands. Grown without synthetic pesticides or fertilizers, organic cotton is kinder to the environment and to the farmers who cultivate it. The chapter delves into the benefits of organic cotton, including its reduced water usage, improved soil health, and lower carbon footprint. Additionally, organic cotton garments are often softer and more breathable, enhancing the wearer's comfort.

Recycled materials are another key component of sustainable fashion. Fabrics made from recycled fibers, such as recycled polyester and nylon, help reduce waste and conserve resources. This chapter discusses the process of recycling textiles, from collecting and sorting old garments to transforming them into new fibers. The benefits of recycled materials extend beyond environmental impact, as they often exhibit enhanced durability and performance.

Innovative fabrics derived from natural sources are gaining popularity in the ethical fashion world. Materials like hemp, bamboo, and Tencel are celebrated for their sustainability and versatility. Hemp, for example, requires minimal water and pesticides, making it an eco-friendly alternative to conventional fibers. Bamboo is fast-growing and biodegradable, while Tencel, made from sustainably harvested wood pulp, offers a silky feel and excellent moisture-wicking properties. This chapter explores the unique qualities of these materials and their potential to revolutionize the fashion industry.

Lastly, the chapter highlights the importance of animal-friendly materials. Ethical fashion seeks to avoid the use of animal products, such as leather and fur, due to concerns about animal welfare and environmental impact. Alternatives like vegan leather, made from plant-based or synthetic materials, offer a cruelty-free and sustainable option. The chapter discusses the advancements in animal-friendly fabrics and their role in promoting compassionate fashion choices.

4

Chapter 4: The Power of Ethical Brands

Ethical fashion brands are leading the charge in transforming the industry. These pioneers are committed to sustainability, transparency, and social responsibility, setting an example for others to follow. This chapter profiles some of the most influential ethical fashion brands and the innovative practices that set them apart.

One of the hallmarks of ethical brands is their commitment to transparency. Consumers have the right to know where their clothes come from and how they are made. Ethical brands provide detailed information about their supply chains, from sourcing raw materials to production and distribution. This chapter explores the importance of transparency and how it fosters trust between brands and consumers.

Fair labor practices are a cornerstone of ethical fashion. Brands that prioritize the well-being of their workers ensure safe working conditions, fair wages, and opportunities for growth. This chapter highlights the efforts of brands that go above and beyond to support their workers, from providing healthcare and education to investing in community development. By prioritizing people over profit, these brands are redefining what it means to be successful in the fashion industry.

Sustainability is at the core of ethical fashion brands. From using eco-friendly materials to implementing zero-waste practices, these brands are committed to reducing their environmental impact. This chapter delves into the various sustainable practices adopted by ethical brands, including upcycling, recycling, and using renewable energy. By embracing sustainability, these brands are proving that fashion can be both stylish and eco-conscious.

Innovation is driving the ethical fashion movement forward. Brands are constantly seeking new ways to improve their processes and products, from developing innovative materials to adopting cutting-edge technologies. This chapter showcases some of the most exciting innovations in ethical fashion, from 3D-printed garments to biodegradable textiles. By pushing the boundaries of what is possible, ethical brands are paving the way for a more sustainable and ethical future.

5

Chapter 5: Embracing a Minimalist Wardrobe

Minimalism is more than just a trend; it's a lifestyle that promotes simplicity, intentionality, and mindfulness. Embracing a minimalist wardrobe is a powerful way to align your fashion choices with your values, reducing waste and promoting sustainability. This chapter explores the principles of minimalism and how they can be applied to fashion.

At the heart of minimalism is the idea of owning less and choosing quality over quantity. A minimalist wardrobe is curated with care, featuring timeless pieces that can be mixed and matched to create a variety of looks. This chapter discusses the benefits of a minimalist wardrobe, from reduced clutter and decision fatigue to a greater appreciation for the items you own. By focusing on quality, you can invest in pieces that are durable, versatile, and ethically made.

Mindful consumption is a key aspect of minimalism. Instead of succumbing to the pressure of fast fashion and constantly chasing new trends, minimalism encourages thoughtful and intentional shopping. This chapter offers practical tips for mindful consumption, from assessing your needs and preferences to researching brands and materials. By making deliberate choices, you can build a wardrobe that reflects your values and supports ethical fashion.

Capsule wardrobes are a popular concept within minimalism. A capsule wardrobe consists of a limited number of carefully selected pieces that can be combined in various ways to create different outfits. This chapter provides guidance on creating your own capsule wardrobe, from identifying essential items to incorporating seasonal pieces. The beauty of a capsule wardrobe lies in its simplicity and versatility, allowing you to make the most of what you have.

Lastly, the chapter addresses the importance of caring for your clothes. Proper maintenance and repair can extend the life of your garments, reducing the need for frequent replacements. This chapter offers tips on caring for different types of fabrics, from washing and drying to storing and repairing. By taking good care of your clothes, you can enjoy them for years to come and contribute to a more sustainable fashion industry.

6

Chapter 6: The Role of Fashion Activism

Fashion activism is a powerful force for change, harnessing the influence of fashion to promote social and environmental justice. Activists, designers, and consumers are using fashion as a platform to raise awareness, challenge norms, and drive positive change. This chapter explores the role of fashion activism and its impact on the industry.

One of the key aspects of fashion activism is raising awareness about the issues plaguing the industry. From environmental degradation to labor exploitation, activists are shining a light on the dark side of fashion and calling for greater accountability. This chapter highlights the efforts of fashion activists who are using their voices and platforms to educate consumers and push for industry-wide changes. Social media has become a powerful tool for fashion activism, enabling activists to reach a global audience and mobilize support for their causes. Campaigns like Fashion Revolution's #WhoMadeMyClothes have sparked conversations about transparency and accountability, encouraging consumers to demand more from brands.

Fashion activism also involves challenging norms and promoting inclusivity. The fashion industry has historically been criticized for its lack of diversity and representation. Activists are pushing for greater inclusivity in all aspects of fashion, from the runway to advertising. This chapter explores the efforts of activists who are advocating for more diverse representation in terms of race, size, gender, and ability. By challenging traditional beauty standards, fashion activism is helping to create a more inclusive and equitable industry.

Collaborations between fashion brands and activists are driving meaningful change. Ethical fashion brands are partnering with activists and organizations to address social and environmental issues. This chapter highlights some of the most impactful collaborations, from joint campaigns to co-designed collections. These partnerships not only amplify the message of fashion activism but also demonstrate the power of collective action.

Fashion activism extends beyond individual actions; it involves systemic change. Activists are advocating for policy changes, fair trade practices, and greater regulation of the fashion industry. This chapter examines the role of advocacy in shaping a more ethical and sustainable fashion landscape. By working with policymakers, activists are striving to create a framework that supports ethical fashion and holds brands accountable.

7

Chapter 7: Circular Fashion: Closing the Loop

The concept of circular fashion aims to create a closed-loop system where products are designed, produced, and consumed in a way that minimizes waste and maximizes resource efficiency. This chapter explores the principles of circular fashion and how they can be implemented to create a more sustainable industry.

At the core of circular fashion is the idea of designing for longevity. Products are created with durability and timelessness in mind, ensuring that they can be worn and enjoyed for many years. This chapter discusses the importance of quality craftsmanship and thoughtful design in creating long-lasting garments. By focusing on durability, circular fashion reduces the need for constant replacements and minimizes waste.

Another key principle of circular fashion is the reuse and recycling of materials. Instead of discarding garments at the end of their life, circular fashion encourages the repurposing and recycling of materials to create new products. This chapter delves into the various strategies for recycling textiles, from mechanical and chemical recycling to upcycling. By closing the loop, circular fashion reduces the demand for virgin resources and minimizes environmental impact.

Circular fashion also emphasizes the importance of responsible consumption. Consumers are encouraged to buy less, choose well, and make their clothes last. This chapter offers practical tips for adopting a circular fashion mindset, from investing in quality pieces to supporting second-hand and vintage markets. By making mindful choices, consumers can play a vital role in promoting a circular economy.

Finally, the chapter addresses the role of innovation in advancing circular fashion. Technological advancements are driving new possibilities for recycling and repurposing materials. From biodegradable fabrics to advanced recycling techniques, innovation is key to making circular fashion a reality. This chapter explores some of the most promising innovations and their potential to transform the fashion industry.

8

Chapter 8: The Rise of Slow Fashion

Slow fashion is a movement that advocates for a more mindful, sustainable, and ethical approach to fashion. It stands in stark contrast to the fast fashion model, emphasizing quality over quantity and promoting a deeper connection to the clothes we wear. This chapter delves into the principles of slow fashion and its growing influence.

One of the core tenets of slow fashion is a focus on craftsmanship and quality. Slow fashion values the skills and artistry involved in creating garments, celebrating traditional techniques and supporting local artisans. This chapter explores the benefits of investing in well-made, high-quality pieces that are designed to last. By valuing craftsmanship, slow fashion encourages a greater appreciation for the work that goes into our clothes.

Slow fashion also promotes mindful consumption. It encourages consumers to be intentional about their purchases, considering the impact of their choices on the environment and society. This chapter offers guidance on adopting a slow fashion mindset, from prioritizing timeless styles to researching brands and materials. By making thoughtful choices, consumers can support ethical fashion and reduce their environmental footprint.

Sustainability is a cornerstone of slow fashion. The movement advocates for the use of eco-friendly materials, sustainable production practices, and minimal waste. This chapter examines the various ways in which slow fashion brands are leading the charge in sustainability, from organic fabrics to zero-waste designs. By prioritizing sustainability, slow fashion is paving the way for a more eco-conscious industry.

Community and connection are integral to the slow fashion movement. It encourages consumers to build a deeper relationship with their clothes, understanding the stories behind them and the people who made them. This chapter highlights the importance of storytelling in slow fashion, from brand narratives to personal experiences. By fostering a sense of connection, slow fashion creates a more meaningful and fulfilling relationship with our clothes.

9

Chapter 9: Ethical Fashion and Cultural Heritage

Fashion is a reflection of culture and heritage, and ethical fashion seeks to honor and preserve these rich traditions. This chapter explores the intersection of ethical fashion and cultural heritage, highlighting the importance of respecting and celebrating diverse cultural expressions.

Traditional craftsmanship is at the heart of many cultural practices. Ethical fashion brands are partnering with artisans and craftspeople to preserve and promote traditional techniques. This chapter delves into the benefits of supporting traditional craftsmanship, from preserving cultural heritage to providing economic opportunities for communities. By valuing and promoting traditional techniques, ethical fashion helps keep these cultural practices alive.

Cultural appropriation is a significant concern in the fashion industry. It involves the unacknowledged or inappropriate use of elements from one culture by another, often for commercial gain. This chapter discusses the importance of cultural sensitivity and respect in fashion, emphasizing the need for proper acknowledgment and fair compensation for cultural contributions. By addressing cultural appropriation, ethical fashion promotes a more respectful and inclusive industry.

Collaboration is key to creating culturally respectful and authentic fashion.

Ethical fashion brands are working closely with communities to co-create designs that honor their heritage. This chapter highlights some of the most successful collaborations, showcasing how mutual respect and shared values can result in beautiful and meaningful fashion. By engaging with communities, ethical fashion fosters a deeper understanding and appreciation of diverse cultures.

Cultural heritage and sustainability go hand in hand. Many traditional practices are inherently sustainable, relying on natural materials and low-impact techniques. This chapter explores the synergy between cultural heritage and sustainability, highlighting how traditional knowledge can inform and inspire modern ethical fashion. By drawing on the wisdom of the past, ethical fashion can create a more sustainable future.

10

Chapter 10: The Role of Technology in Ethical Fashion

Technology is playing a pivotal role in advancing ethical fashion. From innovative materials to cutting-edge production techniques, technology is driving new possibilities for sustainability and ethics in the fashion industry. This chapter explores the various ways in which technology is shaping the future of ethical fashion.

One of the most exciting developments is the creation of sustainable materials through biotechnology. Researchers are developing fabrics made from natural sources, such as algae, mushrooms, and even spider silk. This chapter delves into the potential of these innovative materials, highlighting their environmental benefits and unique properties. By harnessing the power of biotechnology, ethical fashion is pushing the boundaries of what is possible.

3D printing is another technological advancement with significant implications for ethical fashion. This technique allows for the creation of customized garments with minimal waste, as materials are used precisely and efficiently. This chapter discusses the benefits of 3D printing, from reducing waste and transportation costs to enabling personalized and on-demand production. By embracing 3D printing, ethical fashion can reduce its environmental footprint and offer more sustainable solutions.

Blockchain technology is revolutionizing transparency and traceability in the fashion industry. By providing a secure and immutable record of transactions, blockchain allows consumers to trace the journey of their garments from raw materials to finished products. This chapter explores the potential of blockchain to enhance transparency and accountability in the fashion supply chain. By adopting blockchain technology, ethical fashion brands can build trust with consumers and ensure that their practices align with their values.

Finally, the chapter addresses the role of digital platforms in promoting ethical fashion. Online marketplaces and social media are powerful tools for connecting consumers with ethical brands and raising awareness about sustainability and ethics. This chapter highlights the impact of digital platforms on consumer behavior and the growth of ethical fashion. By leveraging technology, ethical fashion can reach a wider audience and drive positive change.

11

Chapter 11: The Importance of Consumer Awareness

Consumer awareness is crucial in driving the ethical fashion movement. Informed consumers have the power to make choices that align with their values and demand more from brands. This chapter explores the importance of consumer awareness and how it can be cultivated to support ethical fashion.

Education is the foundation of consumer awareness. Understanding the impact of our fashion choices on the environment and society is the first step towards making more ethical decisions. This chapter discusses various educational initiatives, from documentaries and books to workshops and courses, that aim to raise awareness about ethical fashion. By educating consumers, we can empower them to make informed choices and support the ethical fashion movement.

Transparency is key to building consumer trust. Ethical fashion brands prioritize transparency by providing detailed information about their practices, from sourcing materials to production methods. This chapter highlights the importance of transparency and how it can help consumers make informed decisions. By being open and honest about their practices, brands can build trust and foster a deeper connection with their customers.

Consumer advocacy is a powerful force for change. Consumers have the ability to influence brands and the industry through their purchasing decisions and advocacy efforts. This chapter explores various ways in which consumers can advocate for ethical fashion, from supporting ethical brands to participating in campaigns and petitions. By using their voices and their wallets, consumers can drive positive change in the fashion industry.

Finally, the chapter addresses the role of media and influencers in raising consumer awareness. Media coverage and influencer endorsements can significantly impact consumer behavior and promote ethical fashion. This chapter discusses the importance of the media and influencers in promoting ethical fashion and how they can use their platforms to raise awareness and inspire positive change.

12

Chapter 12: The Economics of Ethical Fashion

Ethical fashion is not just a moral choice; it's also an economic one. This chapter explores the economic aspects of ethical fashion, from the cost of production to the impact on local economies.

One of the main challenges of ethical fashion is the higher cost of production. Sustainable materials and fair labor practices often come at a premium, resulting in higher prices for ethical fashion products. This chapter discusses the reasons behind the higher costs and the importance of investing in quality over quantity. By understanding the economics of ethical fashion, consumers can make more informed decisions and support brands that prioritize ethics and sustainability.

Ethical fashion has the potential to create positive economic impacts, particularly in developing countries. By supporting fair labor practices and providing safe working conditions, ethical fashion brands can contribute to the economic development of communities. This chapter highlights the benefits of ethical fashion for local economies, from job creation to community development. By choosing ethical fashion, consumers can help create a more equitable and sustainable global economy.

Innovation and efficiency are key to reducing the costs of ethical fashion. This chapter explores various strategies for making ethical fashion more affordable, from technological advancements to economies of scale. By investing in innovation and finding more efficient ways to produce sustainable materials, ethical fashion brands can reduce costs and make their products more accessible to a wider audience.

Consumer demand is driving the growth of ethical fashion. As more consumers prioritize sustainability and ethics, the market for ethical fashion is expanding. This chapter discusses the role of consumer demand in shaping the industry and how it can lead to greater investment in ethical practices. By supporting ethical fashion, consumers can drive positive change and contribute to the growth of a more sustainable industry.

13

Chapter 13: Building an Ethical Fashion Brand

Creating an ethical fashion brand requires a commitment to sustainability, transparency, and social responsibility. This chapter provides a roadmap for aspiring entrepreneurs who want to build their own ethical fashion brand.

The first step in building an ethical fashion brand is defining your values and mission. This chapter discusses the importance of having a clear vision and how it can guide your business decisions. By establishing a strong foundation based on ethics and sustainability, you can build a brand that resonates with conscious consumers.

Sourcing sustainable materials is a crucial aspect of ethical fashion. This chapter provides guidance on finding and selecting eco-friendly materials, from organic cotton to recycled fabrics. By prioritizing sustainability in your sourcing decisions, you can reduce your environmental impact and offer products that align with your values.

Transparency is key to building trust with consumers. This chapter explores the importance of transparency and how to implement it in your business practices. From providing detailed information about your supply chain to being open about your challenges and successes, transparency can help you build a loyal customer base.

Finally, the chapter addresses the importance of collaboration and community. Building an ethical fashion brand is not something you have to do alone. This chapter highlights the benefits of collaborating with other ethical brands, organizations, and activists. By working together, you can amplify your impact and contribute to the growth of the ethical fashion movement.

14

Chapter 14: The Future of Ethical Fashion

The future of fashion lies in ethics and sustainability. This chapter explores the trends and innovations that are shaping the future of ethical fashion and how they can lead to a more sustainable and equitable industry.

One of the key trends is the rise of circular fashion. As discussed in Chapter 7, circular fashion aims to create a closed-loop system where products are designed, produced, and consumed in a way that minimizes waste and maximizes resource efficiency. This chapter delves into the potential of circular fashion to transform the industry and create a more sustainable future.

Another important trend is the integration of technology in ethical fashion. From sustainable materials to blockchain technology, innovation is driving new possibilities for sustainability and ethics. This chapter explores the latest technological advancements and their potential to revolutionize the fashion industry.

Consumer awareness and demand for ethical fashion are continuing to grow. This chapter discusses the role of consumers in shaping the future of fashion and how their choices can drive positive change. By prioritizing ethics and sustainability, consumers can support the growth of ethical fashion and contribute to a more sustainable industry.

Finally, the chapter addresses the importance of policy and regulation in promoting ethical fashion. Governments and policymakers have a crucial role to play in creating a framework that supports ethical practices and holds brands accountable. This chapter explores the potential for policy changes to drive systemic change in the fashion industry.

15

Chapter 15: Ethical Fashion for All

Ethical fashion should be accessible to everyone, regardless of their budget or personal style. This chapter explores ways to make ethical fashion more inclusive and accessible.

One of the main barriers to ethical fashion is the higher cost of production. This chapter discusses strategies for making ethical fashion more affordable, from finding more efficient production methods to offering a range of price points. By making ethical fashion more accessible, brands can reach a wider audience and promote more sustainable consumption.

Diverse representation is crucial for an inclusive fashion industry. This chapter explores the importance of diversity and inclusion in ethical fashion, from the runway to advertising. By promoting diverse representation, ethical fashion can create a more inclusive and equitable industry.

Second-hand and vintage markets are a valuable resource for ethical fashion. This chapter discusses the benefits of shopping second-hand and how it can be an affordable and sustainable option. By supporting second-hand markets, consumers can reduce waste and promote a circular economy.

Finally, the chapter addresses the importance of education and advocacy in making ethical fashion accessible. This chapter offers practical tips for consumers on how to make more ethical fashion choices, from researching brands to caring for their clothes. By raising awareness and promoting ethical fashion, we can create a more inclusive and sustainable industry.

16

Chapter 16: Ethical Fashion and Personal Style

Ethical fashion is not just about making sustainable choices; it's also about expressing your personal style. This chapter explores how you can align your fashion choices with your values without compromising your personal style.

One of the main misconceptions about ethical fashion is that it limits your style options. This chapter discusses how ethical fashion can offer a wide range of styles, from classic to contemporary. By exploring different ethical brands and collections, you can find pieces that reflect your personal style and values.

Mixing and matching is a key aspect of creating a versatile and sustainable wardrobe. This chapter offers tips on how to create different looks with a limited number of pieces. By investing in versatile and timeless pieces, you can build a wardrobe that offers endless styling possibilities.

Accessorizing is another way to express your personal style. This chapter explores how ethical accessories can enhance your outfits and reflect your values. From jewelry made from recycled materials to eco-friendly handbags, ethical accessories can add a unique and meaningful touch to your look.

Finally, the chapter addresses the importance of confidence in expressing your personal style. Ethical fashion is not just about the clothes you wear; it's

CHAPTER 16: ETHICAL FASHION AND PERSONAL STYLE

about how you feel in them. This chapter offers tips on building confidence and embracing your unique style. By wearing clothes that align with your values, you can feel good about your fashion choices and express your true self.

17

Chapter 17: Conclusion: Style with Soul

In conclusion, ethical fashion is about making choices that honor the earth, uphold ethics, and reflect our personal values. This chapter summarizes the key points discussed in the book and offers a final reflection on the importance of style with soul.

Ethical fashion is a journey, not a destination. It requires ongoing effort, awareness, and commitment. This chapter emphasizes the importance of continuous learning and staying informed about the latest developments in ethical fashion. By staying engaged and informed, we can make better choices and support the growth of the ethical fashion movement.

Every choice we make has an impact. This chapter encourages readers to reflect on their fashion choices and consider how they can align them with their values. By making small changes, we can collectively create a significant impact and contribute to a more sustainable and equitable fashion industry.

The future of fashion lies in ethics and sustainability. This chapter envisions a future where ethical fashion is the norm, not the exception. By supporting ethical brands, advocating for policy changes, and raising awareness, we can help create a fashion industry that honors the earth and upholds ethics.

Finally, the chapter celebrates the power of fashion as a form of self-expression and a reflection of our values. Style with soul is about more than just looking good; it's about feeling good and doing good. By embracing ethical fashion, we can create a more beautiful, sustainable, and just world.

CHAPTER 17: CONCLUSION: STYLE WITH SOUL

Style with Soul: How Fashion Can Honor the Earth and Uphold Ethics

In a world where fashion is often synonymous with fleeting trends and mass production, "Style with Soul" takes readers on a transformative journey to discover a more meaningful and sustainable approach to fashion. This enlightening book explores the powerful intersection of style, sustainability, and ethics, challenging the fashion industry to honor the earth and uphold human dignity.

Through 17 engaging chapters, the book delves into the environmental and social impacts of fast fashion, shedding light on the hidden consequences of our clothing choices. It celebrates the rise of slow fashion, circular fashion, and the use of sustainable materials, offering readers practical insights into building a mindful and minimalist wardrobe.

"Style with Soul" also highlights the inspiring stories of ethical fashion brands and activists who are leading the charge for change. It explores the role of technology, consumer awareness, and cultural heritage in shaping a more ethical and inclusive fashion industry. With actionable tips and thought-provoking discussions, the book empowers readers to make conscious choices that reflect their values and contribute to a more just and sustainable world.

Whether you're a fashion enthusiast, a sustainability advocate, or simply someone who wants to align their style with their values, "Style with Soul" offers a refreshing and inspiring perspective on the future of fashion. Embrace the journey towards ethical fashion and discover how your wardrobe can become a force for good.

www.ingramcontent.com/pod-product-compliance
Lightning Source LLC
LaVergne TN
LVHW020501080526
838202LV00057B/6080